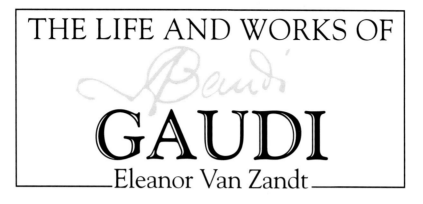

THE LIFE AND WORKS OF

GAUDI

Eleanor Van Zandt

SIENA

The Life and Works of Antoni Gaudí

This edition first published in Great Britain in 1995 by
Parragon Book Service Limited
Units 13-17 Avonbridge Industrial Estate
Atlantic Road
Avonmouth
Bristol BS11 9QD

ISBN 0-7525-1106-8

Printed in Italy

Editors:	Barbara Horn, Alexa Stace, Alison Stace, Tucker Slingsby Ltd and Jennifer Warner
Designers:	Robert Mathias • Pedro Prá-Lopez, Kingfisher Design Services
Typesetting/DTP:	Frances Prá-Lopez, Kingfisher Design Services
Picture Research:	Kathy Lockley

ANTONI GAUDÍ   1852-1926

In the history of architecture, Gaudí stands alone. His vision of what a building might be was personal to a degree matched by no other architect. Although he found inspiration in many styles of building and decoration – including Gothic, Moorish and Art Nouveau – all of these elements were transmuted through his imagination into structures of breathtaking originality.

Antoni Gaudí i Cornet was born in the town of Reus, near Tarragona, in Catalonia. His father was a coppersmith – a fact that no doubt contributed to Gaudí's later mastery in designing metalwork. All his life Gaudí had a reverence for craftsmanship – especially that of his native region. One Catalan speciality was wrought-iron work, and many of Gaudí's most arresting creations are in this medium – often made by his own hand.

At the age of seventeen Gaudí went to Barcelona where, after five years of preparatory courses, he was admitted to the Provincial School of Architecture. Even as a student he showed signs of the eclecticism that he would later take to dizzying extremes. His project for the School's entrance examination was a design for a lecture hall which had a domed ceiling under a stepped, gabled roof and whose walls were decorated with medieval-style tracery. The Neo-Gothic style was then in full flower in Europe and the young Gaudí was an enthusiastic follower of the ideas of the French Neo-Gothic architect and writer Viollet-le-Duc and of the English critic John Ruskin, whose statement 'ornament is the origin of architecture' accorded perfectly with Gaudí's own aesthetic leanings.

Gaudí's first commission after receiving his diploma in 1878 was from the city of Barcelona, for a streetlight design. Although his design was adopted, the city authorities took little further interest in Gaudí's work throughout his career. It was, rather, private patrons, specifically Barcelona's *nouveaux riches*, who warmed to his exuberant style. The city was then experiencing a boom. Large fortunes were being made and large new houses were required. Gaudí's first major completed work was a house for a tile manufacturer, Mañuel Vicens i Montaner. This quasi-Moorish extravaganza took five years to complete, and by the time it was finished, in 1888, Gaudí's career was flourishing. He had already met the man who was to become his principal patron, the textile manufacturer Eusebi Güell i Bacigalupi and was at work on some buildings for his country estate and on Güell's own town house. He had also been approached in 1883 by the Association of the Worshippers of St Joseph and asked to take over as architect of a new church dedicated to the Holy Family. The construction of the Sagrada Familia was to occupy the last year's of Gaudí's life and to be the ultimate expression of the fervent, ascetic Catholicism of his old age.

As a young man, however, Gaudí was a freethinker. A bit of a dandy, he was fond of the company of artists, poets and musicians and frequented the salons of a newly affluent and cultivated middle class, where he was noted for his witty conversation. Although he seems to have had one or two romantic attachments, he never married. Work filled his life almost completely.

As one can imagine from looking at Gaudí's buildings, with their giddy angles, bizarre, organic-looking forms and dazzling colours, he was not the sort of architect to spend hours at his drawing board painstakingly manipulating T-square and compass. He did much of his work on site, improvising as building progressed, testing new shapes and structures with models, discussing his ideas with the construction workers.

Nearly all of Gaudí's work is found in and around Barcelona. This is partly because the demand for it was concentrated in this city – it appealed to the prevailing spirit of the place. Another reason was Gaudí's intense identification with Catalonia. Although he understood Spanish (he had been educated in it), he insisted on speaking only Catalan and considered himself a Catalan, not a Spaniard. Only rarely did he venture outside the borders of his native land, even for professional reasons. In 1908 he was commissioned to design a hotel for New York City but the project never materialized.

From 1914 onwards, Gaudí devoted his entire energies to the Sagrada Familia. As time went on, he became more and more eccentric, living a solitary life in his workshop on the site; occasionally going out, cap in hand, to beg for funds for the church's construction. (It was being financed entirely by contributions.) The church was his obsession. One day while walking the short distance from its building site to a nearby church for vespers, he was hit by a tram. No one recognized him – shabbily dressed as usual – and he was taken, after some delay, to a paupers' ward in a local hospital. Two days later, at the age of seventy-four, he died.

Today, nearly seventy years later, the Sagrada Familia is still a shell, although work on it is progressing slowly. Here and there in Barcelona, his other buildings continue to amaze, shock and delight. Long viewed with amused condescension by architects and critics of the functionalist, modernist school, his work is now being accorded more respect. His eccentricity, playfulness and fantasy are once again being valued and enjoyed.

▽ **Casa Vicens** 1883–88

24 Calle les Carolines

THE INK WAS SCARCELY DRY on Gaudí's diploma when, in 1878, the tile and brick manufacturer Mañuel Vicens i Montaner commissioned him to design a summer residence. The site was then on the outskirts of the rapidly growing city, which has since grown well beyond it. It was not until 1883 that the young architect, with only a few minor projects completed, actually began work on the house. In plan, it was fairly conventional – basically rectangular, positioned perpendicular to the street. But the façade reveals Gaudí's imagination already taking off. The dominant style here is Moorish, with arcades evoking the interior of a Moorish courtyard and with towers suggestive of minarets. Above all, there is a lavish use of tiles – appropriate for the owner (who doubtless hoped that his house would serve as an advertisement for his wares), and a strong Spanish tradition. Although the profusion of ornament may startle Northern European eyes, the house was not quite so unusual in late 19th-century Barcelona, where several of Gaudí's colleagues were then creating similarly extravagant houses for a newly affluent clientele.

◁ **Casa Vicens**
wrought-iron work

GAUDI'S FLAIR FOR DESIGNING –
and executing – decorative iron
work is already evident in the
palm-leaf design of the entrance
gate and fence of Casa Vicens.
The rows of palm leaves, running
in alternating directions, continue
along the top of the low wall in
front of the house. Security was as
much a consideration in 19th-
century Barcelona as it is in big
cities today. The exquisite
wrought-iron grilles over Spanish
ground-floor windows are as
practical as they are decorative,
and Gaudí added some fierce,
albeit slightly curved, spikes along
the top row of palm leaves to
discourage intruders.

◁ **Casa Vicens** fumoir

IN THIS SMALL smoking room
(dating from a period when
smoking was restricted to certain
parts of a house) Gaudí plays with
the Moorish theme of the house.
The light fixture, which is
decorated with Arabic script,
hangs from a vaulted ceiling in a
style typical of Islamic
architecture. Each cell of the vault
– which is made of gold-painted
plaster – is incised to suggest a
palm leaf and bears a cluster of
dates. The walls are lined with
richly modelled papier-mâché.
The deep gold and brown colour
scheme is perfectly complemented
by stained-glass windowpanes in
bright turquoise, a favourite hue
in Islamic art. Needless to say, this
kind of craftsmanship did not
come cheaply, even in those days
of low- paid labour, and Vicens
(not the richest of Gaudí's patrons)
nearly went bankrupt paying
for his house.

▷ **Casa Vicens** gallery adjacent to dining room

LAVISHLY DECORATED ceilings are a hallmark of Gaudí's architecture and this is one of his most complex designs. It combines two *trompe-l'oeil*-painted vaults, suggesting skylights in some sheik's palace, complete with palm branches, with adjacent vaults decorated with shallow designs. Over the door are tiles painted with vivid orange blossoms (also used on the façade). The upper lights of the windows are filled with stained glass of a fairly conventional design. The red stripes against the yellow are probably an allusion to the Catalan flag (itself of red and yellow stripes).

Detail

▷ **Güell Palace** 1886–89

Calle Nou de la Rambla

GAUDI WAS STILL a newly qualified architect when drawings of his work caught the eye of the industralist Eusebi Güell at the Paris International Exhibition of 1878. In the years that followed Güell was to become Gaudí's major patron – as well as a good friend – commissioning from him not only this town house but also some buildings for his country estate, a church (never completed) and a city park, which is today one of Barcelona's main attractions.

The town house (called Palau Güell in Catalan) is a superb building, in which Gaudí's taste for luxury was given full rein. The sober grey stone exterior, however, barely hints at the opulence within – apart from the two grand doorways (Gaudí's favourite parabolic curves) and the flamboyant wrought-iron sculpture between them, which contains allusions to Catalonia's coat of arms. (Güell shared Gaudí's fervent Catalan nationalism.) With its cramped location, partway along a narrow street, the house cannot be seen easily as a whole, although from street level one does get a good view of the projecting first floor, with its stately row of wrought-iron-dressed windows. The regular alternation of their heights gives the façade an almost classical feeling – a quality not often assocated with Gaudí's work.

Detail

▷ **Güell Palace** entrance

AN EXTRAORDINARY FEATURE of
the house is the 'drive-in'
entrance. When guests – or Güell
himself – arrived in their
carriages, they drove straight in
through one of the arches. The
horses were then unhitched and
led down a spiral ramp to the
stables in the basement. A
reference to this equestrian
function of the doorway can be
seen in the curving lines of the
wrought-iron work above the door
– intended to suggest a horse
whip. Just visible inside the
doorway are some of the many
polished marble columns that
endow the house with its majestic
quality. Gaudí made twenty-five
designs for the façade of the house
before he was satisfied with it.

Detail

 Güell Palace   centre hall

THE SPLENDID CENTRE HALL rises from the first floor to the top of the house, a lofty 52 feet (15.86 metres), to create a sense of high drama. Although the floor area is only 27 feet (8.2 metres) square, the various openings – doorways, interior windows, galleries – give it a feeling of spaciousness commensurate with its height. Intended mainly for concerts, the hall is crowned with a dome, and a cupola. The hall shows what Gaudí could achieve given a virtually unlimited budget. The rich materials – polished stone, wrought iron embellished with gold, intricately patterned parquet flooring – are complemented by several glowing paintings by Clapes, another Güell protégé.

Detail

▷ **Güell Palace**
second floor gallery

FROM THIS VANTAGE POINT one
has a fine view of the centre hall
through the wrought-iron railings.
One of the features of the hall is
an organ, with pipes positioned
high above the floor so that music
would float down to the listeners.
It comes as no surprise – given the
grandeur of this theatrical room –
that both Gaudí and Güell were
fond of the music of Wagner. Yet
at the same time the dominant
mood is thoroughly Spanish
(patron and architect would have
said Catalan): grand yet severe
and – with the devotional
paintings – emphatically Catholic.

▷ **Güell Palace** a first-floor salon

THIS VIEW OUT onto the street from the first floor shows some of the parabolic arches that run behind the windows. Made of polished grey snake-eye stone, from the Pyrenees Mountains, they form a counterpoint to the rectangular shapes of the windows and set up a rhythm of their own, running the full width of the house. There are 127 pillars in the house, which serve to heighten its palatial aspect. Note the panels of stained glass to either side of the group of arches.

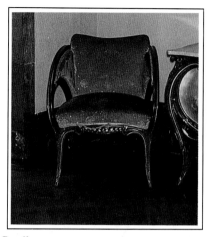

Detail

▷ **Güell Palace** a first-floor salon

GAUDÍ'S INVOLVEMENT with his buildings extended even to the furniture, which he designed himself. This elegant, if rather uncomfortable-looking, sofa, with its attached mirror, end table and lamp, and the matching side chair show him working in the Art Nouveau style – which he would later apply to some of his buildings. Art Nouveau began in the 1880s in Belgium and France. Its sinuous lines, inspired by plant forms, lent themselves well to decorative arts such as wrought iron, glassware and furniture, and the style was quickly taken up and adapted in other countries – for example in the iridescent glass of the American Louis Comfort Tiffany and in the relatively severe version of the style by the Scottish architect and furniture designer Charles Rennie Mackintosh. In Spain the style was called Modernismo, and Gaudí was its foremost exponent – even though he employed it only occasionally.

◁ **Güell Palace**
dining room ceiling

THE STAGGERING COMPLEXITY
and richness of this carved
beechwood ceiling makes it worthy
of a Renaissance prince. The
perforated panels have an
Islamic/Moorish aspect, as do the
eight-pointed star motifs that
decorate both the square grid and
the inner surface of the ceiling.
The judiciously applied gilding
enhances the luxurious effect while
giving greater definition to some of
the elements. Güell made his
fortune in textiles. In 1910 he was
made a count, thus acquiring a
status to match his residence.

▷ **Güell Palace**
rooftop sculpture

DISTINCTIVE ROOFTOPS were to become a Gaudí signature. All sorts of bizarre shapes emerge from the roofs of his later buildings – notably the Casa Milá, where they take on a sinister aspect. In fact, these sculptures have a practical function, serving as chimneys and ventilation ducts (note the holes on the multi-globular shape in the background). Some of them Gaudí decorated with bits of tile in a random pattern – a device he would exploit to the full in the Güell Park. Here, on top of this gravely elegant building, such eccentric objects seem out of place but perhaps the architect felt entitled to indulge his taste for whimsy in a place where they would seldom actually be seen.

◁ **College of Santa Teresa de Jesús** 1888–89

85 Calle de Gandoxer

ANYONE FAMILIAR ONLY with Gaudí's more fanciful work might be amazed to learn that he designed this relatively austere-looking building. Not only a school but also the mother house for the order of Saint Teresa of Avila, the 16th-century mystic, it had to be designed and built with a certain regard for economy and sobriety. Moreover, the ground floor of the College had already been constructed, so Gaudí had to work within an existing plan. Although he kept within the budget, Gaudí was able to indulge his taste for decoration to a modest degree: for example in the attractive patterning of brick and stonework on the façade and in the ceramic plates enclosed by bands of brickwork, which bear the letters I.H.S., representing 'Jesús'. The sharply pointed pinnacles of the parapet and the false arches immediately below enhance the building's ecclesiastical character.

Detail

▷ **College of Santa Teresa de Jesús** main entrance

FOR THE DOORWAY to the College, Gaudí employed one of his favourite structural forms, the parabolic arch. The shape is Gothic in spirit, leading the eye upward, while being unmistakably innovatory. It also provides a graceful frame for the wrought-iron gate, with its cross borne high as if in a procession. The arch is repeated in the ground floor and third floor windows and blind arcading, and inside the building, where a corridor formed of a series of closely spaced whitewashed parabolic arches creates a feeling of serene spirituality, in keeping with the aspirations of the building's inhabitants. The Order of Saint Teresa was founded in 1876 (Teresa herself had been a Carmelite).

▷ **Güell colony** crypt 1898-1917

Santa Coloma de Cervelló

ONE OF GAUDÍ'S most audacious projects is the crypt of a church (never built) intended as the centre of a colony of housing workers from Güell's nearby textile factory. This incomplete work is inspired by Gothic architecture, yet firmly rejects one of its main features, flying buttresses (which Gaudí called 'crutches'), relying instead on slanting pillars as a means of support. One of Gaudí's central tenets was that a structure should stand on its own, as a tree does.

To achieve this, he devised a complicated structural model for this building, consisting of a system of wires from which he suspended little bags filled with buckshot – all proportionate to the size and weight of the actual components of the building. This exterior view shows part of the stairway that would have led up to the church and several of the teardrop-shaped windows which give a haunting, lifelike presence to the broken-brick façade.

◁ **Güell Colony** crypt

THE VIEW OUTWARDS from the entrance to the crypt shows a little thicket of Gaudí's slanting piers and gives a sense of the mysterious, organic quality of this building. None of the piers is exactly like any other, just as no tree is identical to another. The arboreal appearance of the piers is heightened by the freely designed mosaics above them, suggestive of foliage. Note also the curved bricks that Gaudí used for these piers, which give yet another interesting texture to the work.

△ **Güell Colony** crypt

THIS INTERIOR VIEW of the crypt shows some of the roughly hewn basalt pillars that would have formed the main support of the church above, as well as the glowing stained-glass windows – also designed by Gaudí. Slender brick ribs spring from the piers and the arches between them to meet over the heads of worshippers; a similar grouping is positioned over the altar to the right (not visible). In 1915 Gaudí ceased work on this building, leaving it in the hands of his assistant Francesc Berenguer. For the last ten years of his life, his creative energies would be concentrated on the Church of the Sagrada Familia.

Detail

▷ **Bellesguard** 1906-1909

GAUDÍ'S MOST ELOQUENT tribute to Catalonia's medieval past – before it was absorbed into Spain – is this romantic castle, which he built for Doña Maria Sagues. It stands on the site of a manor house built by King Martin I, the last king of Aragon and Catalonia (r. 1396-1410) which bore the same name: Bell Esguard ('beautiful view'). In fact it does enjoy a fine view of Barcelona, to the east. The ruins of this medieval manor remain on the estate today. The newer house, with its rectangular plan and high walls, evokes the formidable keep of the early Middle Ages and Gaudí added a number of details to enhance this effect, notably the slit-like windows and the pretend battlements. However, the characteristically playful idiom in which these are realized actually proclaims the building's 'make-believe' nature. The tower bears one of Gaudí's trademarks: a four-armed cross.

Detail

▷ **Bellesguard** parapet

THE GRACEFULLY TAPERING lines of these mock crenellations (battlements) are a typically inventive Gaudí touch. They punctuate a row of windows which at first glance suggest medieval lancet windows but which are actually sash windows with angular tops. These windows are framed with Gothic-style arcading (interpreted in rough-cut stone). This juxtaposition of contrasting shapes, one in front of the other, was a favourite Gaudí device. The room behind these windows is a spacious hall with an arched ceiling made of unfired bricks. Elsewhere the interior walls are finished with white plaster, which brings a surprising feeling of lightness to the house behind its sober, somewhat forbidding façade. In 1909 Gaudí stopped work on Bellesguard, leaving it to be finished by Domenec Sugranes.

Detail

▷ **Bellesguard** main entrance

BY GAUDÍ'S STANDARDS the decoration of Bellesguard is restrained, even severe, and the roughly cut local stone facing is of a sombre hue. The effect is softened by the relief decoration around the door, which was achieved by placing bits of stone and pottery in moulds and filling the moulds with mortar; the stone remained on the convex surface when the mould was removed.

The two fish mosaics are allusions to Barcelona's great maritime history (note the crowns above them). The city's burgeoning prosperity in Gaudí's time was partly a result of the opening of the Suez Canal in 1869, which greatly stimulated Mediterranean sea trade.

Detail

▷ **Bellesguard** wrought-iron
window box

A CONTRAST OF TEXTURES –
subtle-toned, irregular stone work,
painted wood and spiky wrought
iron – enlivens this window. The
tendrils of iron are appropriate for
a container of plants, while also
providing a measure of security.
The details in Gaudí's buildings
are always integral to the whole
and reflect his love of materials
themselves; their distinctive
qualities and potential.

▷ **Bellesguard** windows

THE GRACEFULLY STEPPED pairing of these two slit windows shows Gaudí at his most restrained. The moulded stone surrounds have a Romanesque aspect and were it not for the curved, twisted pattern of the wrought-iron grilles, these could almost pass for the genuine medieval article. While working on Bellesguard, Gaudí also worked briefly on a real medieval building. This was the Cathedral of Palma in Mallorca (Majorca), which he had been commissioned to restore to something closer to its original appearance – removing some of the accretions of more recent times. Although Gaudí did manage to increase the feeling of spaciousness inside the cathedral – moving the choir stalls out of the nave and into the chancel – and to effect one or two other improvements, his more imaginative ideas did not meet with the clergy's approval. In 1914, he abandoned this project, along with others, and devoted himself thereafter to realizing his own vision of the Gothic style – the Sagrada Familia.

△ **Güell Park** 1900-1914

LOCATED IN THE NORTHWESTERN part of Barcelona, the Güell Park was originally intended as a bold new venture in town planning. Eusebi Güell, an admirer of English landscape design and the new Garden City movement, was resolved to create, in what was then open country, a community in which residents could live in verdant surroundings with a fine view of the city. In the event, only two of the sixty plots were sold and the scheme was abandoned. Nevertheless, Gaudí created some of his most amazing and delightful structures for the Park – which in 1922 was purchased by the city and opened to the public. The site was hilly and rocky. Respecting the terrain, Gaudí avoided levelling it, instead building elevated pathways and tunnels, using the excavated rock as building material. This covered stone walkway is similar in spirit and structure to the crypt of the Güell Colony, though even more coarsely finished, creating the impression of having emerged from the earth – which in a sense it has.

◁ **Güell Park** benches

ONE OF THE BEST-KNOWN features of the park is its long serpentine bench decorated with dazzling mosaics. Gaudí designed some of the patterns himself; the rest he left to the workers. These marvellous abstract patterns almost sing in the sunlight. The form of the bench encourages intimate groupings, as straight benches do not (although Gaudí, who lived in the park for some years, drew the line at physical intimacy and would order demonstrative lovers to move on). In designing the vertical shape of the bench, Gaudí is said to have got a naked man to sit on some still malleable plaster and to have used the resulting impression as a template.

▷ **Güell Park** fountain

AT THE ENTRANCE TO THE PARK Gaudí placed two fountains, each in the form of a monster. In the lower fountain a dragon confronts the visitor; here it is a snake's head, emerging from a red-and-gold-striped banner – an allusion to the Catalan flag. One of the problems Gaudí faced when first planning the park was that it had no natural source of water. His ingenious brain solved the problem with an elaborate system of catching rainwater in a flat open space supported by the pillars shown (page 48) and then filtering the water down through the pillars into a cistern below the fountains.

△ **Güell Park** mosaic

THIS TYPICAL MOSAIC shows the ingenious use of waste tiles, which helped to keep costs down (unusually for one of Gaudí's projects) and which produced hundreds of eye-teasing abstract works of art. The decoration of buildings with tiles (azulejos) is an old tradition in both Spain and Portugal. Gaudí, typically, took this tradition and the ancient tradition of mosaics and, with the help of his workers, created startling patterns in which conventional images – here predominantly scrolls – appear and disappear as if in a kaleidoscope.

△ **Güell Park** entrance

▷ **Güell Park** porter's lodge

THE ENTRANCE TO THE PARK is flanked by two buildings evoking gingerbread houses: an office building and this porter's lodge. On its façade are two plaques bearing the words 'Park' and 'Güell' – the English word being an allusion to the English inspiration behind Güell's original concept, not to the style of its interpretation! The large windows, covered by network-like iron grilles, are framed by red and white ceramic tile surrounds. The 30-foot (9-metre)-high tower, also decorated with mosaics, serves no practical purpose but holds aloft Gaudí's four-armed cross.

THE MAIN ENTRANCE to the park is a hall with quasi-Doric columns supporting a terrace, which was originally intended to serve as the stage of a theatre and as a venue for folk festivals. The severe columns, with their chunky capitals, are a rare instance of a classical influence in Gaudí's work. Paradoxically, he professed to be an admirer of classical architecture, yet a less-classically-inspired architect would be hard to imagine. The ceiling of the hall of columns is decorated with mosaics by Josep M. Jujol, which lend colour to an otherwise rather sombre part of the park. It is these columns through which rainwater is fed into the cistern, supplying the park with water.

△ **Güell Park** detail of porter's lodge

THE WHITE AND coloured ceramic facing on the roof and tower of the lodge enhances the 'gingerbread house' impression with its suggestion of icing. Whereas the windows in the stone-faced part of the tower are more or less conventionally medieval in style, those in the ceramic-faced upper part are wholly original – Gaudí's own notion of what a window in this context might look like. Although Gaudí had his 'signatures', such as the parabolic arch, the leaning pillar and the four-armed cross, he displayed, again and again, a totally fresh approach to form; and it is this that made him so revolutionary – and at the same time an impossible act to follow. The very essence of his art was its element of surprise.

◁ **Güell Park** washerwoman caryatid

AN AMUSING VARIANT on the classical caryatid – an elegant, drapery-clad woman serving as a column – is this rough-hewn washerwoman with her apron and rolled-up sleeves, carrying a basket of laundry on her head, who helps to support the roof of a covered pathway. She may also be Gaudí's tribute to ordinary people who must work hard for a living. Although he had many rich friends, Gaudí never turned his back on his simple origins. While the construction of the park was in progress, he brought his widowed father and niece to live with him there in one of the two houses that had been built as part of the original scheme. This house is now a museum.

Detail

▷ **Casa Batlló** 1905–1907

43 Passeig de Gracia

OTHER EXAMPLES of Art Nouveau seem tame and conventional compared to this fluid fantasy. Is it animal or vegetable? Or perhaps a giant fossil, washed up by the sea? It comes as a surprise to learn that behind this eruption of undulating shapes lies a quite ordinary block of flats, composed of rectangular rooms – apart from the first floor, which was occupied by the building's owner, Josep Batlló i Casanovas. Dissatisfied with the banality of his residence, compared to its more flamboyant neighbours, Batlló engaged Gaudí to liven it up. Gaudí did not disappoint him. The new façade, carved of stone from nearby Montjuic and decorated with small ceramic plates and broken coloured glass, caused a sensation. In Batlló's own flat, Gaudí repeated the curves; walls flow into ceilings, room flows into room. In the words of the architectural historian Henry-Russell Hitchock, they 'seem to have been hollowed out by the waves of the sea'.

Detail

▷ **Casa Batlló**

AT NIGHT, with its fairytale façade
illuminated, Casa Batlló takes on
a magical aura. Of this building
Gaudí himself said, 'The corners
will vanish, and the material will
reveal itself in the wealth of its
astral curves…and it will be like a
vision of Paradise.' In the early
1900s, when electricity was still
quite new, Gaudí could not have
envisaged the dramatic effect that
floodlighting could produce, but
one suspects that he would have
approved of this nocturnal
transformation of his already-
astonishing building into
something not quite of this world.

▷ **Casa Batlló** roof

A SCALY DRAGON – or perhaps a dinosaur – crawls across the top of the building, its scales (overlapping tiles) gleaming in the sun. To reinforce its animal quality, Gaudí has given it a 'backbone' composed of green bead-like pots. In the foreground Gaudí's four-armed cross surmounts a vaguely Russian turret. In the background, clustered chimneys, decorated with tiles, stand like silent masqueraders, observing…. It might be a scene from a fairy tale, and, like most fairy tales, conveys a suggestion of menace.

▷ **Casa Batlló** ventilation shaft

IN STRIKING CONTRAST to the smooth, sensuous curves of the façade, this interior space is decorated with crisp square tiles set diagonally in a regular pattern. However, the curvilinear Art Nouveau theme is re-introduced in the design of the windows; and the shading of the blue tiles, from darker at the top to lighter at the bottom – where less natural light penetrates – softens the overall effect. The regular insertion of textured tiles enlivens the pattern.

◁ **Casa Milá** 1906–10

Passeig de Gracia and Calle de Provença

OFFICIALLY NAMED for its owner, Gaudí's friend Pere Milá i Camps, this massive, surging pile of stone is familiarly known to the citizens of Barcelona as '*La Pedrera*' ('the quarry'). One would assume from its texture that it was made of reinforced concrete – a material that architects a few years later would adopt with great enthusiasm. But Gaudí always remained an advocate of traditional, local materials. Thus the building is made of stone, hammered to produce the desired rough texture. On this occasion Gaudí had plenty of space at his disposal: the total floor area is some 10,000 square feet (926 square metres). The layout of each floor is different from the others; Gaudí did not use load-bearing walls inside the building, but relied on pillars for its support. Once again, he created an undulating roof topped with bizarre chimney sculptures.

◁ **Casa Milá** roof

THIS AERIAL VIEW of the buildiing
shows the flat roof above the
sloping attic storey and the
literally monstrous chimney
figures (compare their size to that
of the attic windows), as well as
the two courtyards that pierce the
building. Originally the walls of
these courtyards were painted
with frescoes, but the colours have
faded badly. These open areas
widen slightly towards the top, in
order to maximize the amount of
light admitted. Below the attic
storey they are surrounded by
hallways. The flats have irregular
plans, full of oblique angles; each
of the building's floors thus
resembles a honeycomb made by
wayward bees.

Detail

◁ **Casa Milá** chimneys

Even in glowing sunlight there is something faintly nightmarish about these figures that dominate the roof of the Casa Milá . Perhaps Gaudí intended them to serve the same function as gargoyles were believed to do on medieval churches: fend off evil spirits. In the light of Gaudí's fanatical piety this is not altogether a preposterous suggestion. Or they may have represented beings from his subconscious mind that haunted his dreams. Gaudí had planned to include, on the façade of the Casa Milá, a figure of the Virgin Mary, with the Infant Jesus and two angels. However an anti-clerical uprising that took place in Barcelona in July 1909 (and which included the burning of a number of monasteries and convents) caused Milá to withold permission for this addition; proclaiming a religious allegiance seemed to be courting trouble. Gaudí did not take this refusal in good grace, and the relationship between him and Milá cooled somewhat.

◁ **Casa Milá** entrance

GAUDI'S MASTERY of wrought iron
is nowhere more evident than in
the marvellous free-form gates he
created for Casa Milá. Two sets of
these gates open onto the two
adjacent streets. Their random
lines are totally modern in spirit,
while retaining the organic quality
so characteristic of Gaudí's mature
work. Their irregularity also serves
to prefigure the irregularity of the
floor plans and so gives added
stylistic coherence to the building.
The building's curved lines recur,
naturally, in the doors – one of
which can be seen to the right of
the gate in this photograph.

△ **Casa Milá** balcony

▷ **Casa Milá** façade

THIS CLOSE-UP PHOTOGRAPH of one of the balconies shows the artistry and originality that went into their design and execution. No two balconies are alike. This is one of the smaller ones. It bursts with vitality – quite different, notes Alfred-Russell Hitchcock, from the 'graceful droopiness' of Hector Guimard's Métro station entrances in Paris, for example. Another architectural historian, David Watkin, likens the ironwork on Casa Milá to 'glistening bunches of seething seaweed'. In fact, the whole building is charged with energy. Even today, after the accomplishment of such architectural feats as the Guggenheim Museum, the Sydney Opera House and the Pompidou Centre, it still has the power to amaze.

ONE WRITER ON GAUDI, Roy McMullen, has described his architecture as 'habitable sculpture'. More than any other of his buildings, Casa Milá exemplifies this image. It appeals to our spirit of play and exploration, the childlike desire to experience new and unusual spatial relations. To live in Casa Milá must be something like living in a giant sand castle. In fact, when it was first built Casa Milá was the colour of sand; eighty years of air pollution have produced its present shade of elephant grey. Although it lacks the magical quality of Casa Batlló, its richly embellished balconies – especially seen through the foliage at street level – do exert a rather imperious charm, like a still-beautiful Spanish dowager wearing a black lace mantilla.

Detail

▷ **Church of the Sagrada Familia** begun in 1882

THE FAÇADE OF THE Church of the Sagrada Familia (Holy Family) shown here, is, in fact, only one of the two transepts, the east or Nativity transept. The other transept, the main façade and the apse – in fact most of this vast edifice – have yet to be built. Before Gaudí was commissioned to design this church in 1883, it had been under the direction of Francisco de Paula del Villar, who planned to build it in the Neo-Gothic style. When Gaudí took over, only the crypt under the apse was (more or less) completed. Following his usual method, Gaudí did not work out the design in advance, but, rather, made sketches of the general form of the building and then improvised the construction and details as he went along. From the outset, however, he was determined not to follow the path of conventional Neo-Gothic architecture. The church was to be Gothic in spirit and in its general form, a Latin cross; but it is clear that Gaudí intended to use his own visual language. His most striking innovation was the four soaring conical towers, which represent four of the Apostles: Barnabas, Simon, Jude and Matthew. The remaining eight Apostles will be represented on the two other façades.

Detail

◁ **Sagrada Familia** interior, east transept

THE INTERIOR of the east transept façade is more conventionally Gothic in design. (Unusually, the church is aligned north-south, rather than with the apse pointing east in the traditional way.) Gaudí made a plaster model of the church, but this was destroyed during the Spanish Civil War in 1936. A new model was constructed but inevitably most of the church – when and if it is completed – will adhere more closely to mainstream Gothic in style. The rose and lancet windows shown here, for example, are quite traditional, apart from the somewhat modern use of three circular lights in the top of each lancet. Gaudí's positioning of a spire over the central portal of the façade will reduce the light entering the rose window. This was probably intentional; Gaudí invested much of his work, especially in later years, with symbolism, but the meanings of most of this symbolism died with him.

Detail

▷ **Sagrada Familia** detail of east transept

THE EAST TRANSEPT is dedicated to the Nativity and events immediately following it. Its three portals are richly incised and encrusted with sculpture – following the medieval tradition but in a spirit more reminiscent of the baroque style. To the left in this photograph we have a depiction of the Flight into Egypt; to the right, Herod's Massacre of the Innocents. The figures in the centre show Saint Joseph instructing the boy Jesus in carpentry. In sharp contrast to the imaginative, fantastic quality of the sculpture on most of his buildings, the figures on this building have an almost photographic realism. In fact they were modelled from photographs, which Gaudí had taken of ordinary people, who suited his purpose better than professional models. In the case of the donkey he went so far as to cover a real donkey, section by section, with plaster of Paris (the donkey survived the experience) and to use this as a lifesize mould for the statue. Such literalism reflects Gaudí the pious Catholic, attuned to the simple faith of most of the worshippers, as opposed to Gaudí the artist.

Detail

▷ **Sagrada Familia** detail of east transept

A RECENTLY INSTALLED STATUE of a harpist adorns the centre portal (the Portal of Love) in the Nativity transept. She is probably meant to be playing for the Christ Child, shown (below centre) being bathed by his Mother, while Saint Joseph looks on. It is the frenetically swirling foliage that gives these portals their real impact. Salvador Dali – himself a master conjuror of unearthly images – spoke admiringly of the 'terrifying, edible beauty' of Gaudí's sculpture. In filling the portals with sculpture, Gaudí was, of course, following an ancient tradition; the porches of medieval churches are thickly embellished with reliefs. In Gaudí's hands, however, these portals seem almost to come alive. A cooling effect is provided by the delicious blue stained glass, whose abstract patterns are reminiscent of Spain's Islamic tradition.

Detail

▷ **Sagrada Familia** west transept

THE WEST TRANSEPT is dedicated to Christ's Passion. Here Gaudí stipulated the use of slanting pillars, which, appropriately, suggest strain, perhaps even the raising of the three crosses on Golgotha, where Christ was crucified. The sculptural tableau at the centre depicts Christ carrying his cross up the hill, his executioners and Saint Veronica, displaying the cloth she gave him to wipe his face on, which bears a miraculous image of it. Unlike the Nativity transept, this one is to be left relatively bare, to intensify the feeling of pain and desolation.

The theme of the main, southern, façade is to be the Glory of God. Gaudí estimated that the church would take two hundred years to build. In his increasing religious fervour, he saw his work as an act of atonement for his sins.

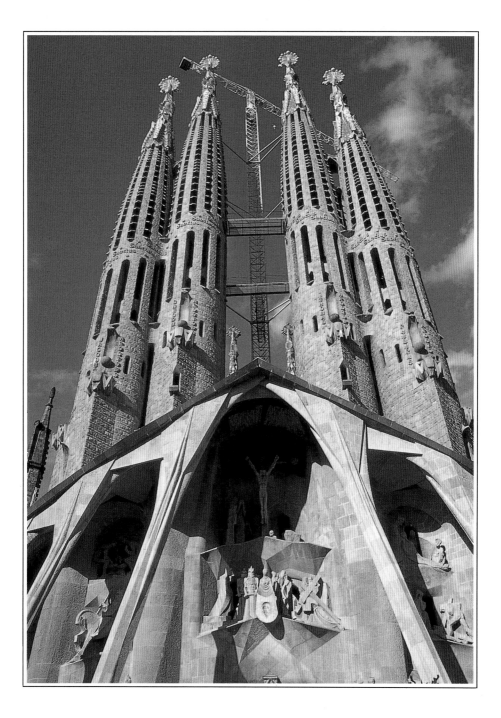

▷ **Sagrada Familia** inside view of a tower

THE DOZENS OF SMALL OPENINGS in the towers and the light streaming in through them create a fascinating interplay of shapes and shadows in the interior of these amazing structures. Here the vertical structural elements are more visible than they are on the outside (whose rough texture unfortunately calls to mind that of a cheese grater). In addition to the twelve 'apostle' towers, the completed church is to have yet more – even taller – towers over the crossing.

◁ **Sagrada Familia** spire

The strange geometric forms and brightly coloured mosaics that adorn this tower are evidence that Gaudí, for all his intense piety, had not lost his love of play. One might easily suppose this to be an ornament from the Güell Park. In fact Gaudí intended the church to be painted – as were, surprisingly, the interiors of medieval churches. For example, the Portal of Hope (Nativity transept) was to be painted green, the colour traditionally associated with this quality. Each of the towers bears words: about half way up, the words 'Sanctus, Sanctus, Sanctus' and, at the top, 'Gloria in Excelsis'.

◁ **Sagrada Familia**

AT NIGHT, with the Nativity transept illuminated from without and within, the church seems a vision of another world – hauntingly, even disturbingly beautiful. Our modern sensibilities, jaded by a glut of sensory input from our everyday surroundings and from films and television, can experience some of the wonder a medieval peasant must have felt when confronted by the glories of a Gothic cathedral, with its jewel-like windows glowing in the light. Whether the Sagrada Familia will ever be finished is uncertain. Some people feel that it should be left unfinished, as a monument to Gaudí. It is hard to see how, even with Gaudí's sketches and the reconstructed model as guides, the builders of today and tomorrow can avoid adulterating his vision – especially given the fact that in any of Gaudí's creations the vision was constantly evolving. Had he lived long enough to complete the church, it would have evolved as he worked on it.

ACKNOWLEDGEMENTS

The Publisher would like to thank the following for their kind permission to reproduce the paintings in this book:

Bookart Architectural Picture Library: 64 **Edifice, London:** 42, 63 **Firo-Foto, Barcelona:** Cover, Half-title, 10, 11, 24, 26-27, 28-31, 33-36, 38-41, 52, 53, 57, 60, 61, 66-69; **Robert Harding Picture Library, London:** 8, 9, 32, 43-51, 54-56, 58-59, 62, 65, 70, 71, 72, 73-78; **The Interior World, London/Fritz von der Schulenburg:** 12-23, 25

Ancient Greek Myths & Legends

AS TOLD BY Philip Ardagh

ILLUSTRATED BY Virginia Gray

Belitha Press

MYTH OR LEGEND?

Long before people could read or write, stories were passed on by word of mouth. Every time they were told, they changed a little, with a new character added here and a twist to the plot there. From these ever-changing tales, myths and legends were born.

WHAT IS A MYTH?

A myth is a traditional story that isn't based on something that really happened and is usually about superhuman beings. The Ancient Greeks called these people heroes. Myths are made up, but they often help to explain local customs, or natural phenomena such as thunder.

WHAT IS A LEGEND?

A legend is very like a myth. The difference is that a legend might be based on an event that really happened, or a person who really existed. That's not to say that the story hasn't changed over the years.

The Ancient Greeks didn't separate genuine history from made-up stories about their past. The two have become so mixed up that it's very difficult to know what is fact and what is fiction.

WHO WERE THE ANCIENT GREEKS?

Greece lies between what is now Italy and Asia Minor. It is made up of a large peninsula – an area of land jutting out into the sea – and a scattering of islands. In about 2000 BC (that's almost 4,000 years ago), different wandering tribes came to the Greek peninsula and settled with the people already living there.

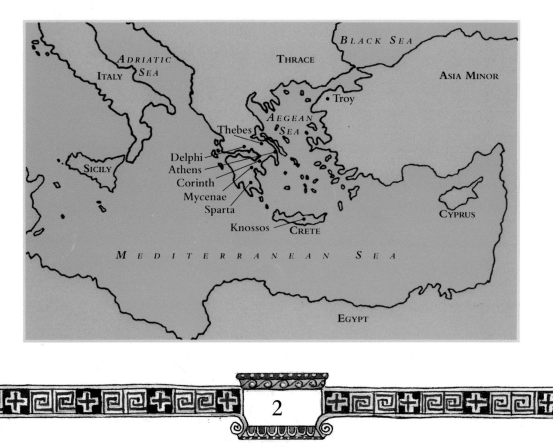

Over time, cities grew, people worshipped the same gods, and the Greeks became a powerful force in Europe. The Ancient Greeks' empire and culture dominated Europe until the Romans took over Greece in 146 BC.

GREEKS AND ROMANS

During Roman rule, Greek influence continued. The Romans even took Greek myths and legends, changed the names of the gods and heroes, and used them as their own. For example, the Greek hero Heracles simply turned into the Roman hero Hercules!

HOW DO WE KNOW?

Greek myths and legends began to grow in the 8th century BC, when the poems of a Greek poet named Homer became popular. The oldest surviving written works in Greek literature are two epic poems called *The Iliad* and *The Odyssey*, both of which are said to have been written by him. They tell of the siege of the city of Troy and of the adventures of the hero Odysseus.

STATUES AND CARVINGS

Many characters in Greek myths and legends survive as statues and as carvings on ruined buildings. They also appear on pots. These are often painted in two styles: Attic black figures – black figures on a reddish-orange background; and Attic red figures – red figures on a black background. The illustrations in this book are loosely based on these Ancient Greek styles.

The jar and vase above are painted in the Attic style and show scenes from Greek myths and legends. The central figure on the jar at the top is Dionysus, the Greek god of wine.

GODS, GODDESSES & HEROES

There are many Greek gods and goddesses, as well as heroes, kings, queens, monsters and ordinary men and women. Greek gods and goddesses were immortal and could live forever. They were said to live on Mount Olympus which is a real place in Greece. Here are some of the characters you will meet in this book. The names given to them by the Romans are shown in brackets.

ZEUS (Jupiter) King of the gods, and god of thunder and lightning. Quick-tempered and often turns against humankind.

HERA (Juno) Goddess wife of Zeus. Also quick to take offence.

HERACLES (Hercules) Hero son of Zeus, but not Hera. He had to complete twelve tasks, or labours, in his efforts to become one of the gods on Mount Olympus.

DIONYSUS (Bacchus) God of wine. Carries a staff with vines wrapped around it.

ATHENA (Minerva) Goddess of war. This terrifying warrior used her cunning to help the hero Perseus kill Medusa.

APHRODITE (Venus) Goddess of love. Very beautiful and easily angered.

POSEIDON (Neptune) God of the sea. Uses his three-pronged spear, or trident, to make storms and control the waves.

HADES, sometimes called PLUTO (Dis) God of Tartarus, the Underworld of the dead, which is sometimes called the Kingdom of Hades.

HERMES (Mercury) Messenger of the gods. Wears winged sandals.

PROMETHEUS Cleverest of the gods and a friend to humankind.

PERSEUS Hero whose most famous adventure was his quest to kill Medusa, the Gorgon.

THESEUS Hero who faced the Minotaur – half bull, half beast – and freed its victims.

PANDORA The first woman. She was sent down to earth by the gods, and opened a jar which she'd been told to leave well alone. Out of it poured all the evil and troubles of the world.

BELLEROPHON Hero who rode through the skies on the back of the winged horse, Pegasus.

PARIS Trojan hero who snatched Helen and took her to Troy.

HELEN OF GREECE, later of TROY The most beautiful woman in the world. She was seized by Paris and taken to Troy. This is the event that led to the Trojan wars.

The Ancient Greeks carved images of the characters in their myths and legends on the walls of their buildings. At the Temple of Athena in Paestrum (above) there are carved scenes of Greek heroes fighting in the Trojan wars.

ODYSSEUS (Ulysses) Hero of Homer's *Odyssey* and many adventures.

JASON Hero leader of the Argonauts. He had a ship called the *Argo*.

OEDIPUS Tragic hero, doomed from birth. He killed his own father and married his mother.

NOTE FROM THE AUTHOR
On the following pages you will find some of the most famous Ancient Greek myths and legends. They can be read on their own or one after the other, like a story. Mostly, they are fun and exciting, even though they can be gruesome or sad in places. I hope that you enjoy them and that this book will make you want to find out more about the lives of the Ancient Greeks as well as their myths and legends.

ORPHEUS Musician who followed his wife Eurydice to the Underworld of the dead to plea for her life.

MIDAS AND HIS GOLDEN TOUCH

The story of a man who fulfilled a prophecy and whose dream came true... but then became a dreadful curse.

Before King Midas was even a king of Phrygia – in fact, when he was still a little baby – he was left lying in the garden of his parents' palace. When it was time for his nursemaid to bring him out of the sun and into the cool of the palace, she let out a yelp of surprise.

There was a row of ants crawling up the baby prince and each one was holding a golden grain of wheat. In turn, each ant popped a golden grain into the baby's mouth, then made its way back down his body.

The nursemaid snatched up the young Midas, frantically brushed the remaining ants off him, and ran indoors to tell his parents what had happened. Rather than being upset as she'd expected, they were delighted at what she told them.

'This is a good omen!' said Midas' father. 'I'm sure of it.'

'We must go to the soothsayers to find out what it means,' his mother agreed.

The soothsayers, who could see into the future, agreed with Midas' father. This was indeed a good sign. Golden wheat meant that real gold was to come. One day, Midas would be a very rich man.

When Midas was old enough to understand, his parents told him of his future good fortune, but he soon forgot about it... Until one day, Dionysus, the god of wine, offered to grant him a wish.

Gods didn't usually grant humans wishes, but Midas had found Dionysus' friend, Silenus, in his garden. He'd been left behind after one of the god's fantastic parties. Midas made sure that Silenus got back to Dionysus safely, which was why Midas was being offered a wish.

The king thought long and hard about what he wanted...

Suddenly, he remembered the omen of the golden grains of wheat. 'Let everything I touch turn to gold!' he said, with greedy excitement.

'Are you sure that's what you want?' grinned Dionysus, taking a gulp of wine and smacking his lips together with delight.

'Yes!' cried Midas, without a second thought.

'Then it is granted,' said Dionysus. 'Don't say I didn't warn you.'

Midas bent down and picked up a twig. The moment his fingertips touched the wood, it turned to solid gold. Then he tried a leaf, a clump of grass... an apple. Now he was enjoying himself! Hurrying back to his palace, he touched each marble column and they too turned to gold.

Midas sat down at the dinner table for a celebration feast, but it soon turned into a famine. When he reached out and touched a piece of bread, it turned to gold and he couldn't bite into it. When the wine in his golden goblet reached his lips, it too turned to solid gold and couldn't be drunk.

Hungry and thirsty, Midas rose to his feet and paced up and down the marble floor in his golden sandals. Just then, his young daughter ran into the room.

'Hullo, daddy,' she beamed and, before he could stop her, she threw her arms around him. The minute she touched her father the king, she turned into a solid gold statue.

Midas hurried, weeping, to find Dionysus. 'Please release me from this curse,' he begged. 'My greed got the better of me!'

'Very well,' said the god of wine, with a chuckle. 'There is a way to undo this magic,' and he told the king what he had to do.

Following these instructions, Midas hurried to the source of the river Pactolus – the place where the water springs from the ground near Mount Tmolus – and washed himself.

Two things happened instantly: he was freed from the curse of his golden touch, and the sands on the bed of the river Pactolus turned a beautiful gold, which is why they are that colour to this very day.

Medusa ~ the Snake-Haired Monster

With her hair of writing serpents, just one glimpse of the terrifying Medusa could turn you to stone.

Medusa was one of three monsters called the Gorgons. They had the bodies of women, snakes for hair, teeth like the tusks of wild boars, sharp claws and wings of gold. Anyone who dared to look in the face of a Gorgon was turned to stone in horror.

The young hero Perseus was on a quest to kill Medusa. Fortunately, he had the help of the gods. Athena, the goddess of war, went with him on his journey. Hermes, messenger of the gods, gave him a sharp knife to cut off her head. Some nymphs gave him a pair of winged sandals so that he could fly, a magic helmet to make him invisible, and a special pouch to keep Medusa's head in if he was successful.

One final gift was from Athena herself. She handed Perseus a shield.

'It contains no magic, but it is vital to your task,' she explained.

'It's beautiful,' said Perseus, admiring the gleaming shield. The bronze was so highly polished that he could see his face in it.

'Use it as a mirror,' said the goddess, and the young hero understood.

Entering the place where the three Gorgons slept, Perseus squeezed through the silent crowd of stone victims. He knew that if he was to so much as glimpse Medusa's face, he too would become a lifeless statue.

He turned his face to one side and held his shield up in front of it, reflecting the sleeping Medusa in the shield's polished surface. Then, with his eyes fixed firmly on the shield, he made his way over to her sleeping form. He pulled out the knife Hermes had given him, and cut off Medusa's head without ever having to look at the hideous creature.

In this way, the world was rid of one more terrifying monster and Perseus earned his place among the heroes.

THE MAN WHO LOVED HIMSELF

The word 'narcissistic' describes people who
spend a lot of time admiring how they look.
It comes from the name Narcissus, who is
the main character – though hardly
a hero – of this legend.

There's no denying that Narcissus was very beautiful or handsome
or both. Many people came to him and declared their undying
love for him, but he treated them all in the same way – he rejected
them. He wanted nothing to do with them, because he thought that
he was far too beautiful to be seen with them.

He decided that the person he would share his life with would
have to be *at least* as beautiful as he was and, in his opinion, that
person would be very hard to find!

One day, Narcissus was walking through the forest when he felt
sure he was being followed.

'You show yourself!' he shouted.

'*You* show *yourself*!' a voice replied. The words were the same as his,
but Narcissus thought the voice was even more beautiful than his own.

'Come here,' he pleaded. 'Let me see you.'

'Let *me* see *you*,' the strange voice sighed.

Captivated by her voice and the fact that she – whoever she
was – thought and spoke in such a similar way to him, Narcissus
cried: 'Let me hold you!'

'Let *me* hold *you*!' replied the voice, with obvious joy, and out of
the trees came a nymph called Echo.

She threw her arms around Narcissus but, when he saw that she was
nothing more than an ordinary nymph, he pushed her roughly away.

'I could never love you!' Narcissus screamed, with a cruel smile.

'Love you,' said Echo with great sadness. She longed to tell Narcissus just how much she loved him, but was unable to speak of her feelings. In the past, Echo had upset Zeus with all her talking, so he punished her by taking her own speech away from her. All she could do was repeat what had just been said.

Rejected by Narcissus like all others before her, Echo left the forest with great sadness, but she still loved him.

Time passed and, one day, Narcissus came to a clear, pure spring filling a pool at Donacon in Thespia. He sat on the grassy bank and looked into the water. There he saw a perfect reflection of himself in all his beauty… and promptly fell in love with it.

When he realized that the most beautiful person he had ever seen was himself, he decided that life wasn't worth living any more. He pulled out his dagger and, with a final cry of 'goodbye', plunged it straight into his heart.

'Goodbye,' sobbed Echo, who still so loved Narcissus that she had followed him and was hiding nearby.

Where Narcissus' blood touched the ground, a single white flower sprouted from the earth which is named narcissus after him. But unlike the man, the flower is not aware of its own beauty.

The Minotaur in the Maze

King Asterion of Crete had no children of his own, so he adopted three brothers. When he died, one of the brothers, Minos, seized power. This was just the beginning of a tale that would lead to death, destruction and despair.

Minos said that he'd offer up a prayer to the gods to try to prove to everyone that he was the rightful ruler of Crete. He claimed that, if the gods answered his prayer, this would prove beyond any doubt that they were happy for him to be king.

'What shall I pray for?' he asked a crowd outside the palace.

'Pray that a great white bull comes charging out of the sea!' someone shouted, saying the first unlikely thing that came into his head.

'And if this prayer is answered?' demanded Minos. 'Am I then your rightful king?'

A cry of 'Yes!' rang out through the crowd, and Minos was overwhelmed with joy.

Now, Poseidon is the god of the sea so, if Minos wanted a great white bull to come charging out of it, he'd have to pray to Poseidon. But how could he tempt Poseidon into answering his prayer?

King Minos was a very crafty person. He knew that there was nothing the gods liked more than an animal sacrifice. This was when an animal was killed in their name and offered up to one of them. The more spectacular the animal, the greater the honour to the god. Minos would pray to Poseidon for the bull and promise to sacrifice it to him afterwards.

So Minos built an altar to the god of the sea and prayed for a sacrificial bull to come charging out of the waves...

And so it did. The pure white beast burst to the surface and swam to the shore. When the crowds saw this, they could see that the gods were on Minos' side and that he must surely be their rightful ruler.

But there was still the matter of sacrificing the bull. It was the most impressive bull Minos had ever seen. He couldn't bring himself to kill this marvellous animal, so he broke the promise he had made to Poseidon in his prayer. He sent for one of the bulls from his herd and sacrificed that instead.

Poseidon felt cheated. In revenge, he made Pasiphë, Minos' wife and queen, fall in love with the bull and there was nothing she could do about it.

Minos was delighted when Pasiphë said she was going to have a baby, but the delight soon turned to horror when the child was born: it was half human and half bull. Minos wasn't the father – the bull was. Horrified and ashamed at the disgrace he had brought on his family by betraying Poseidon, King Minos hurried to an oracle – a kind of soothsayer – to ask what he should do.

'How can I avoid the scandal and dishonour?' he asked.

'Ask the craftsman Daedalus to build you a palace at Knossos,' replied the oracle. 'Hide your shame with cunning.'

King Minos took his advice, and asked the famous inventor and designer, Daedalus, to build a palace with the most complicated maze underneath. He called this maze the Labyrinth.

The Labyrinth was a place of endless corridors and winding passages, with many a dead end and only one true path to and from the centre. At its very heart, King Minos hid Pasiphë and the monster with the man's body and bull's head – away from the prying eyes of the people of Crete. Pasiphë named her grotesque son Asterius, but as he grew up, he became known as the Minotaur.

Now, King Minos once had a much-loved son called Androgeus, but he had been killed by the Athenians – people from Athens – who were ruled over by King Aegeus.

To make up for his son's death, Minos was sent seven young men and seven young women from Athens as a tribute every nine years.

The tribute came to the island of Crete in a ship rigged with a black sail. The young men and women were led into the winding passages of the Labyrinth. It was impossible for them to find their way out. There were too many twists and turns in the dark, shadowy tunnels. Alone and frightened, all they could do was to wait for the Minotaur to catch the smell of human flesh in the air...

When he reached them, the terrifying half-beast tore them to pieces, crunching their bones and eating them raw! The echoes of their cries rang through the Labyrinth.

When it was time for the Athenians to send their third tribute, eighteen years after the first, Theseus, King Aegeus' own son, offered to be one of the seven men to go. His father was horrified.

'Don't worry,' Theseus tried to reassure him. 'We will keep your promise and send King Minos his tribute, but I also promise that all fourteen of us shall return home safely.'

'Then take this white sail with you, my brave son,' said King Aegeus. 'If the ship returns without you, let the black sail remain rigged to the mast. If you succeed in your task, rig this white one. Then I will know of your victory and safe return before you even reach our shores.'

'It's a white sail you shall see,' his son assured him.

Once the tribute had been chosen, Theseus secretly let two of the young women go and replaced them with two boys. King Aegeus would keep his promise: the Minotaur would indeed be sent fourteen Athenians, but not all would be as it seemed...

When Theseus and the tribute arrived on the shores of Crete, King Minos was there to greet them. At his side stood his daughter, Ariadne. No sooner had she laid eyes on Theseus than she fell in love with him. When her father turned his attention elsewhere, Ariadne whispered to Theseus: 'I will help you kill the Minotaur.'

'But how will I find my way in the Labyrinth?' Theseus whispered.

'I know a way,' said Ariadne, 'and I will show you if you promise to take me back to Athens and marry me.'

'I promise,' said Theseus, mouthing the words in silence as King Minos turned back to him.

'Tonight, you are my prisoners,' said the king. 'Tomorrow, you meet the Minotaur. Now come.'

That night, Ariadne met secretly with Theseus and handed him a magic ball of thread. 'This was given to me by Daedalus,' she explained. 'It was he who built the maze beneath the palace. Tie the loose end of the thread to the door post as you enter the Labyrinth, then drop the ball on the floor. It will lead you to the Minotaur.'

'And there I will kill it!' hissed Theseus.

Ariadne nodded. 'Once this is done, pick up the ball, rolling up the thread as you go, and it will lead you back to the entrance.'

Armed only with a sword given to him by Ariadne, Theseus entered the Labyrinth alone that night. As Ariadne had instructed, he tied one end of the thread to the door post, then dropped the ball to the floor. Like any ball of thread it began to unravel but – *unlike* any other – it made its way along the passages that led towards the centre... and to the Minotaur.

Meanwhile, under the cover of darkness, the Athenian men overpowered the guards outside their room. The women were having equal success. The two boys who had disguised themselves as women took their guards completely by surprise, killing them quickly and quietly. Now all they could do was wait.

While the others waited, Theseus made his way along the twisting tunnel, barely able to see the ball of thread unrolling silently at his feet. The flickering light from the flaming torches gave the Labyrinth a strange orange glow, and there was a smell of death in the air. Then, suddenly, the ball came to a standstill and Theseus became aware of the heavy breathing of an animal. The Minotaur was asleep!

Theseus raised his sword, just as the Minotaur opened one eye.

The creature leapt up to face him. With one swift motion, Theseus slashed off the Minotaur's head, then followed the thread back to the entrance. While it was still dark, he joined the others. Ariadne guided them back to their ship and they slipped out of the harbour.

No one knows for sure the reason why but, despite everything Ariadne had done for him, Theseus broke his promise to her. When they stopped for a few days at the island of Dia, later called Naxos, he left her there, sleeping, and travelled home without her.

No one can say for certain, either, why Theseus forgot to take down the black sail and rig the white one. Perhaps he was so pleased with his success… or perhaps he was saddened at having betrayed Ariadne. Whatever the reason, the black sail remained fluttering on the rigging of the ship as it pulled into the harbour.

Watching from the clifftops, his father, King Aegeus, saw the sail was not the white one. He took this to mean that his son had died in his attempt to kill the Minotaur. With a cry of despair, he threw himself from the cliffs and drowned in the sea that is now called the Aegean in memory of him.

PROMETHEUS' GIFT TO HUMANS

According to some myths, it was the god Prometheus who created the human race. No wonder he wanted it to thrive.

One day, when an argument arose over which part of an animal should be sacrificed to the gods and which part should be kept by humans, Zeus called in Prometheus to judge. Knowing that Zeus always thinks 'bigger is better', Prometheus took a dead ox and separated the meat from the bone and fat. Next, he squeezed the meat inside a small parcel, and the bones and fat together inside a much larger one. He took the two parcels to Zeus.

'You choose,' Prometheus said to the king of the gods and, just as he'd guessed, Zeus chose the bigger parcel... And that is how it came to be that humans eat the meat, while the less pleasant fat and bones are offered up to the gods.

Zeus found out he'd been tricked and was furious. 'Humans may keep the meat,' he bellowed, 'but I'll not give them the fire to cook it!'

Prometheus thought that this was most unfair. He secretly went up to Mount Olympus, and lit a torch from the flames of the fiery chariot of Helios, the sun god. Quickly, he snapped a piece of glowing wood from the torch and hid it in the middle of a vegetable called fennel. Then he slipped away and came down to earth where he shared the secret of fire with our ancestors.

When Zeus learned what had happened, he had Prometheus chained, naked, to a pillar in the Caucasian mountains. Here, every day and all day, a vicious, hungry eagle tore at his liver until it was eaten. Every night, the liver would grow again ready for the following day's torture. There Prometheus remained until he was rescued by Heracles, the greatest hero of them all.

ICARUS ~ THE BOY WHO REACHED TOO HIGH

Daedalus was one of the greatest inventors of his day, but he could not control his jealous rage, or the recklessness of his son Icarus.

Daedalus lived in Athens and was famous for his clever inventions. People came from far and wide for his advice and ideas on how to make things. He had a young nephew, called Talos, who helped him with his work. Very soon, Talos became a better inventor than he was, and people began to ask him for advice instead of asking Daedalus.

Daedalus put a stop to this once and for all when, in a fit of jealousy, he pushed Talos from the roof of the temple of Athena. With Talos dead, Daedalus left Athens in a hurry – which was how he came to settle on the island of Crete.

Unfortunately for Daedalus, he fell out with King Minos after Theseus killed the Minotaur. The angry king threw the inventor into the Labyrinth along with his son, Icarus.

With help, they escaped from their prison, but how could they escape from the island? It wouldn't be long before they were tracked down and locked up again. Daedalus soon came up with a plan. He trapped birds, and used their feathers to build two huge pairs of wings. He sewed the feathers on to cotton and sealed them in place with wax. He then strapped one pair of wings to his son and the other to himself.

'If we jump off that high ground together, Icarus, and you do as I do, we'll escape from this island with our lives,' said the old man, 'but there are a few simple rules we must follow.'

'Yes, yes,' said Icarus, impatiently. He was anxious to leave before anyone discovered them.

'Listen!' said his father. 'You mustn't fly too high or too low. Simply follow me and do as I do.'

Then, after a silent prayer to the gods, Daedalus launched himself off the ground and soared through the air. The wings worked! They really worked! He was flying!

Soon father and son had left the island of Crete behind them, but it was not long before Icarus forgot his father's words of warning.

This was such fun! A cool breeze blew from the sea below. The sun warmed them from above. The sky was a beautiful clear blue. The further they flew, the more carefree and careless Icarus became.

He soared, he swooped, he dived through the air and then flew up and up and up, until he was far too close to the sun. The heat of the sun's rays melted the wax that held the feathers in place. The wings began to fall apart...

'Father!' cried Icarus. 'Father! Help me!'

But Daedalus was too far ahead to hear his son's cries. It was only when the inventor heard a loud splash in the calm waters below that he realized what had happened. Icarus had hurtled to his death in the waters near the island of Samos.

Daedalus had been punished by the gods for pushing his nephew Talos from the temple roof. As he flew to safety, his tears fell from the skies and into the sea, where his son Icarus had met his tragic fate.

PEGASUS ~ THE WINGED HORSE

When Perseus cut off the head of the terrifying Medusa, a winged horse leapt from her dead body. This was Pegasus, a beautiful and brave creature.

Night after night, Bellerophon dreamed of the wonderful winged horse that he'd seen drinking at the spring at Peirene. Every morning he'd wake up and wish that this beautiful steed could be his. One night, the dream changed. The goddess Athena appeared to him and handed him a golden bridle.

'With this, Pegasus shall be yours,' she told him. So the horse had a name: Pegasus. Bellerophon woke with the word on his lips. In his hands, he felt something cold and he looked down to see that he was clutching a golden bridle. This had been no ordinary dream.

Bellerophon hurried back to Peirene and there, sure enough, Pegasus came in to land. He crept forward, and slipped the magic bridle on to the horse. Pegasus' eyes met his, and each understood the other.

The hero and the winged horse had many adventures together. For a while, Bellerophon lived in the palace of King Proitos of Argos. Unfortunately, the queen fell in love with him, but he felt nothing for her. Hurt by his rejection, she went to her husband, King Proitos, and claimed that it was Bellerophon who was in love with her.

Saddened by the news, the king sent the unsuspecting Bellerophon to deliver a message to King Iobates of Lydia. The message was sealed shut and Bellerophon had no idea that it was his own death warrant. It requested that Iobates kill the messenger who brought it.

When the king read the message, he didn't want blood on his hands. He decided the best way to kill Bellerophon was to send him on an impossible quest. His kingdom was plagued by the Chimaera, a fire-breathing monster, with a lion's head, a goat's body and a serpent's tail.

'You must kill it for me, Bellerophon,' he said, fully expecting him to become the Chimaera's next victim.

But Bellerophon was cunning as well as brave. Riding on the back of Pegasus, he swooped down on the beast and thrust a spear deep into its throat. The end of the spear was made of lead which melted in the heat of the monster's fiery breath. The molten lead then poured down the Chimaera's throat, burning its insides and killing it.

King Iobates was so pleased at being rid of the Chimaera that he chose to ignore King Proitos' request. He not only let Bellerophon live, he also let him marry his daughter and have half of his kingdom.

In time, Bellerophon became more and more self-important. He thought that he was the greatest hero of all time and was very full of himself. One day he decided that he was equal to the gods, and would fly on Pegasus to Mount Olympus to claim his rightful place there.

Zeus would have none of it. He sent a single gadfly to bite Pegasus. The winged horse reared up in surprise, throwing its rider from its back. Bellerophon fell to earth with a bump and spent the rest of his days as a poor outcast.

Today, Pegasus lives with the gods on Mount Olympus, carrying Zeus' thunderbolts on its back.

THE TWELVE LABOURS OF HERACLES

There are many heroes in the myths and legends of Ancient Greece, but none is more popular than Heracles.

Heracles was the son of Zeus and a woman called Alcmene, whom Zeus had tricked into loving him. Zeus' wife, the goddess Hera, hated Heracles from the start. She sent two giant, venomous serpents to kill Heracles when he was just a baby... But Heracles was no ordinary child. The following morning, Alcmene found her son happily cooing in his cot, holding the two dead snakes that he'd strangled with his bare hands – not only saving his own life, but that of his half-brother too.

Heracles grew into a handsome man of incredible strength. He could fight well with all types of weapon, but his favourite was a club that he had cut and shaped from an olive tree.

Zeus had originally planned that Heracles would become King of Mycenae but, because she had been so badly betrayed, Hera had made sure that the honour went to Heracles' cousin, Eurystheus.

She did agree that if Heracles could succeed at twelve special tasks set by King Eurystheus, then he would be entitled to become one of the immortal gods of Mount Olympus.

These tasks were the twelve labours of Heracles. Each was designed to be impossible, for Hera didn't want Heracles to succeed.

The first labour was to kill the Nemean lion – a lion whose skin was so thick that no weapon could pierce it. Heracles tried with his sword and his club, but each attempt failed. In the end, he wrestled with the mighty beast and strangled it as he had the serpents as a baby.

Heracles returned to King Eurystheus. He wore the lion's skin to prove that he'd been successful. He'd found that the only way he could skin the lion was by using one of its own claws as a knife.

Eurystheus was amazed and a little frightened to see Heracles. He'd expected news of Heracles' death to reach him, not Heracles himself!

'And what is my second labour, cousin?' asked Heracles, beaming.

'To kill the Hydra,' said Eurystheus, trying to hide a triumphant grin. Surely even the great Heracles wouldn't survive this challenge?

The Hydra was a many-headed monster that lived in the swamplands of Lerna. The creature was said to be immortal, as each time you struck off one of its heads, two more grew in its place. The goddess Hera made sure that this labour was even harder for Heracles by sending an enormous crab to lurk in the swamp and nip at his legs.

But Heracles had a plan. Every time he cut off one of the Hydra's heads, his cousin, Iolas, touched a flaming torch to the stump of the neck. This stopped the blood from flowing and new heads from growing. Finally, with the last head chopped off, and the last stump scorched, the Hydra lay dead.

Now that Heracles had proved successful at killing beasts, Eurystheus gave him a labour that would mean that the hero had to bring one back alive.

He was sent to capture the Ceryneian Hind – a deer of great grace and beauty with golden antlers. The deer could run at great speed, and it took Heracles a year before he caught it in Arcadia. This was a sacred animal so, rather than tying it up or harming it, Heracles pleaded with the goddess Artemis to command the creature to go with him to the king. Artemis agreed... so Eurystheus had to set him a fourth, near-impossible task.

There was a wild boar destroying crops and farm animals around Mount Erymanthos. It was a fierce animal and the local people were more than a little frightened of it. It had become known as the Erymanthian Boar, and Heracles' fourth labour was to capture it. This he managed to do by cornering the boar in a snowdrift and binding it with rope. He then carried it back to King Eurystheus on his shoulders.

Heracles marched into the palace with the boar held high. It is said that when the king saw the beast with its huge tusks, he was so frightened that he scuttled off his throne and hid in a large brass jar!

Then came the fifth labour. All Heracles had to do was to clean out the Augeian Stables. This sounds simple enough, but Heracles had one day to do it, and the stables had never been cleaned. They were piled high with horse manure and cattle dung.

Heracles completed this task in an ingenious way. Using his superhuman strength, he dug trenches which diverted the water from two nearby rivers and washed the stables clean!

On the shores of Lake Stymphalos was a flock of the most dreadful birds you can imagine. They had razor-sharp beaks and claws and wings of metal. They not only hunted and ate the animals that stopped to drink at the lake, but they also ate humans. Heracles' sixth task was to rid the world of them all.

When Heracles arrived, he found that he could kill the odd one or two Stymphalian birds when they were in flight. An arrow fired from his bow could pierce their underbellies. The trouble was that most of the flock were roosting in the trees, and no shouting or clapping would make them leave the safety of the branches.

Fortunately for Heracles, not all the goddesses were on Hera's side. The goddess Athena, a daughter of Zeus, gave Heracles a special bronze rattle to help him in his task.

The rattle proved very useful. Every time Heracles shook it under the trees, the birds took flight and Heracles could shoot them down. In this way, he completed his sixth labour.

Next, Heracles had to capture the Cretan Bull. This was the same bull that Poseidon had given to King Minos for him to sacrifice, but which he'd kept for himself. This huge, white bull was now on the loose in Crete, killing any islanders who crossed its path. But it was no match for Heracles. He brought it back to Eurystheus, who wanted to offer it as a sacrifice to Hera.

But because her enemy Heracles had caught it, the goddess wanted nothing to do with the bull.

This brings us to the eighth labour of Heracles – to capture the flesh-eating horses of the terrible King Diomedes of Thrace. Heracles killed the evil king and, while the horses of Diomedes were busy feeding off their own master, he herded them together and drove them to Mycenae. One thing we can be certain of – Eurystheus must have been horrified when he saw them.

Heracles was proving to be so successful at his tasks that when Eurystheus' daughter said that she longed to own the Girdle of the Amazon, the king decided to see if Heracles could bring it back as his next labour. The girdle was a piece of bronze armour, worn by Hippolyta, queen of the mighty race of warrior women. Whether he had to kill her for it, or whether she willingly gave it to him as one warrior to another, isn't really clear, but – yet again – Heracles returned triumphant.

This left just three labours. The tenth was to bring the Cattle of Geryon back to Mycenae. Geryon wasn't a place, it was a giant and no ordinary giant at that. It had three heads, six arms and a weapon in each hand – but still Heracles defeated it and managed to herd the cattle to Eurystheus.

Heracles' eleventh task was to collect the Golden Apples of the Hesperides. On his journey, he found the chained Prometheus suffering endless attacks from the eagle, as his punishment from Zeus. Heracles killed the bird, set Prometheus free, then went on his way.

Only gods or goddesses were allowed into the garden of Hesperides where the apples grew, so Heracles had to ask Atlas to go in for him. It was Atlas' job to hold up the heavens, so Heracles had to hold them for him while he picked the apples.

'I'll take the apples to the king for you,' said Atlas on his return. 'I'm tired of holding up the heavens, and you can do it just as well as me.'

'That's fine,' said Heracles, thinking quickly.

'Before you go, would you hold the heavens for me, for just a moment, while I make a pad for a sore spot on my shoulders? If I'm taking over your task, I need to be as comfortable as possible.'

Atlas put down the apples and held up the skies once more.

'Thank you,' Heracles grinned. He snatched up the apples and was off on his way, leaving the tricked Atlas fuming with rage.

This left Heracles one last task. If he could succeed in this twelfth labour, then he had earned the right to become a god. This time, he had to enter the Underworld itself. He was to bring the king the dog which guarded the entrance to Tartarus. Cerberus was no ordinary dog. It had three dogs' heads, a mane of writhing snakes, and a serpent's tail, but it could do nothing against Heracles' brute strength.

When Eurystheus came face-to-face with the dog from hell, he was almost speechless.

'T–T–T–Take i–i–i–it b–b–b–back,' he spluttered, running from the room in horror.

Heracles had successfully completed the last of his twelve labours. No one could deny his right to become a god and to take up his place on Mount Olympus.

ODYSSEUS AND THE ONE-EYED GIANT

**A hero of many adventures, Odysseus had
to use quick wit, strength and cunning
to defeat Polyphemus the Cyclops.**

Odysseus had been away from home for ten long years when he
visited the island of the Cyclopes. These were terrifying giants
with a single eye in the centre of their foreheads. They tended sheep,
which they ate whole.

Odysseus and some of his men entered a cave and rested and
sheltered there. It was the home of a Cyclops called Polyphemus, who
was one of the sons of the sea god Poseidon. When evening came, the
one-eyed giant returned with his flock. With his sheep safe inside, the
huge and hideous creature rolled an enormous stone across the mouth
of the cave. It was so big and so heavy that no human – no *team* of
humans – could hope to move it. Odysseus and his men were trapped.

Catching sight of the frightened humans, Polyphemus the Cyclops
snatched up two of Odysseus' crew and swallowed them whole. The
next morning, he ate another two, then rolled back the stone to let his
sheep out. He couldn't believe his luck – he had a larder full of humans!

'What is your name, little man?' asked the giant, as he stepped out
of the cave and began to roll the rock back across the opening.
'Are you one of these heroes I hear so much about?'

'Me, a hero?' laughed Odysseus. 'I am a nobody.' Then an idea
began to form in his mind. 'In fact, my name is Nobody.'

'Greetings, Nobody. I look forward to eating you on my return,'
grinned the Cyclops, as the giant boulder blocked out the sun.

That night, Polyphemus returned with his sheep and – as Odysseus
watched helplessly – snatched up another two men and ate them.
Then the Cyclops drank some wine, and fell into a deep sleep.

Odysseus didn't waste any time. He pulled out a huge wooden stake, which he'd hidden out of sight in the shadows, heated the point in the fire, then climbed on to the sleeping giant's chest. With all his might, he thrust the stake into Polyphemus' single eye. The giant screamed, loud enough to bring the other Cyclopes to the outside of his cave.

'Are you all right, Polyphemus?' cried one, through the rock across the entrance. He didn't want to roll it aside in case Polyphemus was simply having nightmares... and he wouldn't be too pleased if all his sheep escaped for no reason!

'Are you under attack?' asked another Cyclops, aware that strangers had been seen on the island.

Remembering the name that Odysseus had told him, Polyphemus shouted out, 'Nobody's hurting me!'

Misunderstanding Polyphemus' cries, and satisfied that he was in no danger, the other Cyclopes returned to their parts of the island.

'Nobody's hurting me!' the Cyclops cried, expecting help to arrive.

The next morning, blinded but not defeated, Polyphemus felt his way along the stone walls of his cave. He rolled the huge rock just far enough for a single sheep to pass through.

'I'll let my sheep out to graze one at a time, Nobody,' he declared. 'But you and your men will remain here until I decide to eat you. I don't need to see to eat – just a hearty appetite and sharp teeth.'

As each sheep passed through the gap in the cave opening, Polyphemus stroked its fleece to check that it really was a sheep and not a human trying to slip past him.

Imagine his surprise, therefore, when he heard Odysseus' voice outside his cave.

'You should have thought to feel underneath the sheep,' he bellowed. 'We strapped ourselves beneath their bellies.'

Just to make absolutely sure that the Cyclops knew who had outwitted him, he added, 'And I am certainly not a nobody. My name is Odysseus. Remember it well!'

ORPHEUS AND THE UNDERWORLD

**The story of a man's music that brought tears
to the eyes of the dead and gave a beautiful
nymph a second chance to live.**

Orpheus played the lyre so beautifully that the birds in the air,
the fish in the water, and the animals above and below ground
would come to listen to his music.

This wonderful gift made him very happy but his wife, the nymph
Eurydice, made him happier still.

Try to imagine then, his utter horror when Eurydice stepped on
a poisonous snake which bit her foot. The poison quickly took effect,
and Orpheus could see her life draining away from her.

Orpheus followed his wife down to Tartarus – the world of the dead
ruled over by Hades and his queen, Persephone. He pleaded with them
to let his wife live again and played them some sad music. So powerful
was this music that it made the dead forget their woes and cry for him.

'Your music speaks to me,' said Hades. 'Its sadness tells of a true love,
so I release Eurydice to you. Go now, and she will follow, but don't
look at her until you reach the surface, or she will be lost to you.'

Bursting with joy and declarations of thanks, Orpheus dashed up
to the world of mortals, hearing Eurydice's footsteps behind him.

When he could see daylight ahead he wanted to sing for joy! 'Nearly
there,' he said, turning to her. He had forgotten Hades' command and
Eurydice fell back into the Underworld never to be seen again.

Orpheus spent his days in the forest, but all the tunes he played
were sad ones. Those who looked after him soon became jealous of
his undying love for the dead nymph, and they decided to kill him.
His grave is said to be easy to find because a nightingale hovers over
it, forever singing to his memory.

THE WOODEN HORSE OF TROY

The exciting thing about a surprise present is that you never know what might be inside. That can also be the danger.

According to Greek legend, the war between the Greeks and the people of Troy was a long and bloody one, and at the centre were Helen, the most beautiful woman in all of Greece, and Paris, the Trojan prince who loved her.

Paris was the son of the King and Queen of Troy. When he was born, his mother dreamed that she was giving birth to a flaming torch. Fearful that this was a bad omen, King Priam ordered that the child be left on a hillside to die.

Luckily, Paris was found by a group of shepherds who brought him up. He led a remote life, away from the influence of others, and this is why he was called upon by the goddesses Hera, Athena and Aphrodite to settle an argument about which of them was the prettiest.

Each goddess tried to bribe Paris to choose her. Hera promised him power, while Athena offered him the skills to make him a fine warrior. But it was Aphrodite's bribe that he couldn't resist. She said that, if he chose her as the prettiest, Paris would win the love of the world's most beautiful woman, Helen of Greece. So Paris declared Aphrodite the winner, instantly making enemies of the other two goddesses.

Paris went to Sparta, convinced that Helen would fall in love with him. He snatched Helen from her husband and took her back to Troy.

A huge fleet of Greek heroes set sail to Troy to try to bring her back. When words failed, they laid siege to the city.

After nine long years of war, someone in the Greek ranks hatched a plan and built a huge, hollow, wooden horse on wheels. Some say it was the hero Odysseus' idea. Others say that it was Epeius' master plan.

One morning, the sentries at the gates of Troy woke to find the extraordinary horse left outside. The next thing they noticed was that the Greek armies had gone. Reports soon reached Troy that the Greek fleet had been seen sailing away. The war was over!

A captured Greek soldier claimed that the horse had been built as an offering to the goddess Athena so that she might give them the wind for their sails.

Helen who, as Aphrodite had promised, now loved Paris with all her heart, was suspicious of the wooden horse, but none of the Trojans would listen to her. They wanted to bring this offering to Athena inside the walls of the city.

That night, while the city slept, the Greek fleet came silently back to the shore and the armies made their way to the walls of Troy. Inside the city, there was a movement from within the horse. It was full of Greek soldiers who had been hiding there all the time!

They opened a trap door in the horse's belly, lowered a rope ladder and climbed down under the cover of darkness. Overpowering the sentries, they opened the gates and let in their comrades.

There were some dreadful deeds done that night, ending with the city of Troy being burned to the ground. The dream of Paris' mother that he was a flaming torch had indeed been a terrible omen.

JASON AND THE ARGONAUTS

Jason, heir to the throne of Iolcus, had come to claim his crown. First he had to fetch the Golden Fleece from a magical ram – a task intended to destroy him. Aboard his ship, the *Argo*, Jason and his crew had many adventures.

'Good luck, Jason!' shouted a voice in the small crowd which had gathered on the shore to see Jason off on his quest. The *Argo* floated proudly on the dawn waves, its brilliant white sail glowing orange in the light of the rising sun.

On its crowded decks stood Jason and his forty-nine-strong crew, the Argonauts. Never before had such a brave and heroic crew sailed together in one vessel. It included everyone from Heracles the hero, to Atlanta the huntress. Jason raised his hand in salute to the crowd.

Many had expected Heracles to captain the *Argo*, but he insisted that Jason should be in charge of the ship as well as the quest for the Golden Fleece at Colchis.

Their first stop was at the island of Lemnos, where Jason and the Argonauts were greeted by fierce, helmeted warriors shaking spears. When Jason managed to convince them that his mission was a peaceful one, the warriors removed their helmets. They revealed themselves to be beautiful women dressed in their dead husbands' armour.

Jason soon discovered that Lemnos was inhabited entirely by women. They had murdered all the men – except for one who was set adrift in a boat without oars – because the men had treated them badly.

The Lemnian woman were very welcoming and eager for the Argonauts to stay and marry them. It was a long time – some say a year – before Jason's crew managed to return to their ship.

Soon, the Argonauts were hurtled into further adventures...

They were forced to leave Heracles behind at a place called Arcton. Heracles and another Argonaut had gone in search of a third who had been lured to an underwater grotto by love-sick nymphs. A good wind had come up and Jason was forced to set sail without them.

In Thrace, the Argonauts visited King Phineus, who had been blinded by the gods for being too good at seeing into the future. Despite his blindness, Phineus still had the gift of soothsaying, and Jason wanted to ask his advice about what lay ahead for him and his crew of Argonauts.

'I will tell you what you need to know,' replied Phineus, his sightless eyes staring ahead into nothingness. 'But first you must rid me of the curse of the Harpies.'

'What are they?' asked Jason.

The blind man smiled. 'You shall soon see,' he said. 'Dine with me.'

Soon, a vast banquet was laid out before Jason and his ship's company. Just as King Phineus reached for a piece of bread, the air in the hall was filled with the sound of beating wings and screams of hideous laughter.

Jason looked up and was shocked to see two terrifying, winged women swoop down and snatch food from Phineus' table. Again they swooped, then yet again, snatching up the food.

'These are the Harpies,' sighed Phineus, 'and I am dying of hunger because they will not let a morsel of food pass my lips.'

Jason called across the table to the Argonauts, Calais and Zetes.

'Help Phineus so that he might help us,' he cried.

The two Argonauts nodded, bade their friends farewell, then flexed their wings – for they were sons of Boreas, the North Wind – and flew up after the Harpies, chasing them from the palace.

With the Harpies gone, Phineus was free to eat and drink at last. When he'd had his fill, he kept his promise to Jason. He told him everything that might help him on his journey, including how to deal with the Symplegades Rocks at the entrance to the Bosphorus Sea.

Finally, the Argonauts said goodbye to the soothsayer king and climbed back aboard the *Argo*.

With the wind behind them, Jason and his remaining Argonauts finally reached the Symplegades Rocks. They loomed out of the sea mists before them like a pair of sentinels. Between the two rocks was a narrow passage of water which they would have to row down.

Unlike many an unwary seafarer who had gone before them, Jason's crew had the advantage of Phineus' knowledge. He had warned them that these rocks moved. They smashed together, crushing any unsuspecting thing that passed between them.

'Release the dove,' Jason instructed, working to Phineus' plan.

As the bird flew between the rocks, the Argonauts watched carefully to see how quickly they came together to try to crush the creature. They watched the path the dove took and the speed with which it flew. It had just completed the journey, when the rocks crashed together, catching a few of its tail feathers.

'We must row as fast as the dove flew,' Jason announced. 'Any slower and we'll lose more than our tail feathers!'

So the sail was lowered, and the Argonauts took up their places at the oars, then rowed between the Symplegades Rocks at a speed no one has rowed before or since. Even then, they only just made it. There was a splintering of wood, as the very tip of the stern of the *Argo* was crushed and torn away, and the rest of the ship passed safely through.

Now it was on to Colchis, where King Aeëtes held the Golden Fleece. Here, the gods – who so often like to meddle in the affairs of humans – decided that it would be good sport to make the king's daughter, Medea, fall in love with Jason.

On hearing of Jason's quest, Medea's father agreed to let him have the fleece, so long as he fulfilled some near-impossible feats.

'Firstly, you must hitch my two fire-breathing bulls to a plough,' he commanded. 'And then you must plough the great Field of Ares for me.'

'That is a huge field, your majesty,' said Jason. 'It will take days.'

'You have only one,' said the king. 'And that is not all. You must sow dragons' teeth in the freshly-tilled soil, and face the consequences.'

The other Argonauts gasped. No single person could complete such a difficult task, and who knew what might grow from dragons' teeth?

'And, if I succeed, the Golden Fleece is mine?' asked Jason, staring into the face of King Aeëtes.

'You have my word,' the king nodded, knowing in his heart that the fleece was safe, for the man who stood before him was bound to fail.

What he hadn't bargained for was that his own daughter, Medea, would help Jason. Hopelessly in love with him, she gave Jason a special ointment that would protect him from the bulls' fiery breath, and any weapons he might encounter – but only for a day.

Jason smeared the magic ointment all over himself, then faced the bulls and yoked them to the plough. Although the ointment protected him from harm, he used his own brute strength and determination to harness the beasts and to plough the Field of Ares in a day.

Night fell, and it was time for Jason to sow the dragons' teeth. No sooner had the last handful fallen into the rich, tilled soil, than they grew into hundreds upon hundreds of armed soldiers.

As quick as a flash, Jason used an old trick. He snatched up a stone and threw it at the back of the head of one of the soldiers. The dazed soldier spun around and began to fight the man behind him. Soon the squabble spread and the soldiers were fighting each other rather than turning their attention to Jason. Swords were drawn, spears were thrown and, after much bloody in-fighting, every man lay dead.

Jason had accepted the king's challenge and – with a little help from Medea – he had been victorious. The Golden Fleece was rightfully his, but Aeëtes had no intention of keeping his word.

Unaware of her love for Jason, the king told his daughter that he planned to kill Jason and the Argonauts. Medea hurried to Jason and led him to a sacred grove where the Golden Fleece hung from a tree.

This precious prize was guarded by a famous dragon of a thousand coils – a dragon which could not be killed.

'That terrible beast is bigger than my ship!' gasped Jason. 'How can I hope to get past it to the fleece?'

'Dragons are relatives of the snake, and all snakes can be charmed,' said Medea, and she began to sing a strange and wonderful song, with magical and soothing words.

As the dragon's eyelids began to droop, Medea stepped forward slowly and sprinkled sleeping dust in its eyes. No sooner were the dragon's eyes completely shut than Jason dashed forward and pulled the Golden Fleece from the branch.

Safely back on the *Argo* with Medea and his Argonauts, Jason set sail to claim the throne of Iolcus. Even then his adventures were not over. It took more of Medea's trickery to help him win the crown...

Though Jason had many more adventures, his death was not a hero's death. He betrayed Medea and, at the end of his life, he was sad and lonely. Sitting by the now-old *Argo*, remembering past glories, he was struck on the head and killed by a timber from the ship that had carried him into legend.

OEDIPUS ~ DOOMED BY PROPHECY

The gods can be cruel at times and they certainly were to Oedipus. Even before he was born, he was condemned to be a murderer, and worse...

According to myth, when Pandora opened a jar and let disease and despair into this world, she also released Hope, the one thing that makes the lives of mortals bearable when times are hard. But there was no hope for Oedipus. Even before he was born, Apollo prophesied that he would grow up to kill his own father.

When Oedipus' father, King Laius of Thebes, heard this, he panicked. 'We must kill the baby as soon as it is born,' he said.

'No!' cried Queen Jocasta. 'He will still be our son, and to kill him would be to go against the prophecy of the gods! Who knows what troubles we might bring down upon the whole kingdom of Thebes!'

'Then we must send him away,' said the king. 'If he perishes, that is the will of the gods...' He smiled to himself. He would make *sure* that the baby perished, even if he didn't actually kill him.

'And if he survives?' sobbed Jocasta.

'If he survives, he'll have no idea who his father is and the prophecy may yet fail!' said the king.

When the baby was born, Jocasta just had time to give him his first kiss before he was snatched by his father, the king. Laius strode from her bed chamber and – out of sight of his sobbing wife – tied up the bawling infant and nailed his feet together with a spike.

'Take him to Mount Cithaeron,' he ordered a servant, 'and leave him there to die.'

Too frightened to go against the word of his arrogant master, the servant did as he was told. There is no way of knowing what thoughts were in his mind as he carried out this dreadful deed.

Perhaps it was chance that he left the child near a flock of sheep. Perhaps it was the will of the gods that a shepherd discovered the baby. He was a poor but kind man, who tended the boy's wounds and named him Oedipus, which means 'swollen foot'. He took the child to the palace at Corinth, knowing that King Polybus and Queen Periboea were kind people and didn't have any children of their own.

King Polybus and his queen treated the child with love and kindness, and Oedipus grew into a fine prince, but not a happy one. As a young man, he looked nothing like the king and queen – whom he thought of as his mother and father – and he felt very out of place.

He decided that he should go to an oracle at Delphi, who was famous throughout Greece for her advice and wisdom, and see whether she could explain his strange feelings.

'What makes me stand out from others?' he asked.

'Go!' said the oracle.

'No,' insisted Oedipus. 'I must know.'

The message the oracle gave him was a shattering one.

'You will kill your father and marry your mother!' she boomed.

Thinking that Polybus and Periboea were his father and mother, Oedipus was horrified. They were such loving parents! He swore never to return to Corinth and never to see them again. That way they would be safe from him.

With great sadness, Oedipus began to travel aimlessly from land to land. One day, he was walking down the road, his scarred feet aching, when a horse reared up in front of him.

'Out of my way, you lowly scum!' a voice bellowed. The horse was pulling a chariot carrying an angry, red-faced man. 'Out of my way!'

Until that moment, Oedipus had had every intention of stepping aside to let the chariot pass, but something in the man's voice made him stand his ground. There was no need for such rudeness.

When Oedipus refused to move, the man in the chariot cried out with an uncontrollable rage and tried to run him down.

Oedipus managed to leap aside, safe from the thundering hoofs and crushing wheels. He lunged at the man, who toppled off the back of his chariot and became entangled in his horse's reins. The last sight Oedipus had of the man was of him being dragged behind the chariot in a cloud of dust, his broken neck caught in the reins.

What Oedipus had no way of knowing was that this was King Laius, his true father. The first part of the prophecy had come true.

Shaken by the man's rage and horrific death, Oedipus went on his way. He arrived in the outskirts of Thebes to find it in turmoil. A large Sphinx – half lion, half woman, with eagle's wings – had taken up position at the entrance to the city. Everyone who tried to pass her was presented with a riddle.

If the passers-by could answer it, they were free to pass into Thebes. If they failed, she killed and ate them. The riddle remained unchanged because, so far, no one had been able to answer it correctly. The number of dead was rising and fear had spread throughout the city.

Oedipus knew nothing of this, so was shocked to be confronted by the strange beast. 'Answer me this riddle,' she demanded, 'What walks on four legs in the morning, two legs at midday and three legs at night?'

Oedipus thought long and hard. Whereas other people had been frightened, and quick to give any answer in the hope that it was the right one, Oedipus took his time.

'By morning, you could mean the early years,' said Oedipus slowly, looking into the frightening eyes of the Sphinx for clues as to whether he had the right idea. Her eyes were expressionless.

'By midday, you could mean the middle years,' he continued.

'What is your answer?' snapped the creature.

'And by evening you could mean the last years of life,' said Oedipus.

'Your answer?' the Sphinx screeched.

'A human,' said Oedipus. 'In his youth, he crawls on all fours. As an adult, he stands upright and walks on two legs but, as he gets older, he needs a third leg – a walking stick – to help him.'

'Yes! Yes! Yes!' wailed the Sphinx, the words turning into a mournful cry as she flew up Mount Phicium and hurled herself – wings unopened – to the valley below, smashing herself to death on the rocks.

Freed from the curse of the Sphinx, and learning of the death of the hated King Laius, the people of Thebes made Oedipus their king in grateful thanks. His wisdom had saved them from the monster.

To seal the authority of his kingship, Oedipus then wed Laius' widowed queen, Jocasta, unaware that he was fulfilling the prophecy of the oracle at Delphi. He was now married to his own mother.

Neither knowing the other's true identity, the new king and queen of Thebes were very happy and, over time, had four children. Then a terrible plague came to the land. People died, crops failed and the water turned sour. It was almost as though Thebes and its people were being punished by the gods.

Oedipus returned to the oracle at Delphi to seek advice. 'How can I rid my kingdom of this terrible plague?' he asked.

'By casting out the murderer of Laius,' replied the oracle.

When Oedipus returned to Thebes he declared that whoever had murdered King Laius should be sent into exile, unaware that he was the murderer!

The truth was revealed when blind Teiresias, the most famous soothsayer in all of Greece, had an audience with Queen Jocasta.

'You have news of how to save our people?' she asked.

'I have news that may well save the people of Thebes, but it is not news that will please you, your majesty,' said Teiresias.

'You speak in riddles,' said the queen. 'If you can help us stop this awful plague, please tell me what you know.'

'It was Oedipus who killed your husband, Laius,' said the soothsayer.

'You lie!' screamed Jocasta, leaping to her feet. 'The prophecy said that our own son would kill him, and Oedipus is the son of Polybus and Periboea of Corinth.' She sent a messenger to Corinth to be sure.

'No. He's not our child,' Queen Periboea told Jocasta's messenger.

'Oedipus was brought to us by a shepherd, his tiny feet spiked together and bleeding, but we brought him up as our own son. We have never known who his real parents were.'

On hearing this news, Queen Jocasta summoned the servants and found the one who had taken her baby son to the mountainside all those years ago, on the orders of King Laius.

His head bowed in shame, the servant spoke of the baby boy. 'His hands were tied and his tiny feet were spiked together,' he confirmed.

Jocasta thought of Oedipus' feet and their distinctive scars. Teiresias, the blind soothsayer, was right... Oedipus really *was* her son and she was married to him!

Horrified and shamed, Queen Jocasta hanged herself. Oedipus was filled with such a mixture of hopelessness and rage that he blinded himself, realizing that it had been impossible to escape the prophecy. He spent the rest of his life as a wandering beggar.

The sadness of this tale is that nothing was the fault of Oedipus. He was lucky in one thing, though. However sad he was, and wherever he travelled thereafter, his daughter Antigone went with him, because she truly loved her father.

INDEX

First published in the UK in 1997 by

Belitha Press Ltd
London House, Great Eastern Wharf,
Parkgate Road, London SW11 4NQ

Copyright in this format
© Belitha Press 1997
Text copyright © Philip Ardagh 1997
Illustrations copyright © Belitha Press 1997
Philip Ardagh asserts his moral right to be
identified as the author of this work.

ISBN 1 85561 725 0

British Library Cataloguing in Publication
Data for this book is available from the
British Library.

Series editor: Mary-Jane Wilkins
Editor: Julie Hill
Designer: Jamie Asher
Educational consultant: Liz Bassant

Printed in Hong Kong